It's Halloween!

by Richard Sebra

LERNER PUBLICATIONS ◆ MINNEAPOLIS

Note to Educators:

Throughout this book, you'll find critical thinking questions. These can be used to engage young readers in thinking critically about the topic and in using the text and photos to do so.

Lerner Publications Company
A division of Lerner Publishing Group, Inc.
241 First Avenue North
Minneapolis, MN 55401 USA

For reading levels and more information, look up this title at www.lernerbooks.com.

Library of Congress Cataloging-in-Publication Data

The Cataloging-in-Publication Data for *It's Halloween!* is on file at the Library of Congress.
ISBN 978-1-5124-1430-1 (lib. bdg.)
ISBN 978-1-5124-1503-2 (pbk.)
ISBN 978-1-5124-1504-9 (EB pdf)

Manufactured in the United States of America
1 – VP – 7/15/16

Expand learning beyond the printed book. Download free, complementary educational resources for this book from our website, www.lernerresource.com.

Table of Contents

Trick-or-Treat

Halloween is a fall holiday.

People celebrate it on October 31.

Halloween began as a harvest festival.

It marked the start of winter.

What kinds of foods might be at a harvest festival?

Halloween started

in Europe.

Later it came to the

United States.

People dress up in costumes.

Some are scary.

Some dress as ghosts and witches.

What are some other costumes people might wear?

Kids like to trick-or-treat.

They walk from house to house.

People give them candy.

Some people put up

decorations.

They may have

scarecrows.

They may have

spiderwebs.

Pumpkins grow in the fall.

People cut faces into them.

They put candles inside.

The pumpkins glow.

People scare each other

on Halloween.

They tell ghost stories.

What are other kinds of scary stories?

It is fun to dress up.

Halloween is a great time

to be with friends.

Pumpkin Carving

Pumpkins can have many faces.
They can be happy, silly, or mean.

Picture Glossary

costumes

clothes you wear to pretend to be someone else

decorations

things you put around a house on a holiday

glow

to shine or light up

harvest

a time when food is taken from farms

Index

Read More

Felix, Rebecca. *We Celebrate Halloween in Fall.* Ann Arbor, MI: Cherry Lake Publishing, 2013.

Pettiford, Rebecca. *Halloween.* Minneapolis: Jump!, 2016.

Smith, Mary-Lou. *Celebrate Halloween.* New York: Cavendish Square Publishing, 2016.

Photo Credits

The images in this book are used with the permission of: © demarco-media/iStock.com, p. 5; © Candus Camera/Shutterstock.com, pp. 6, 23 (bottom right); © spectrumblue/Shutterstock.com, pp. 8–9; © kali9/iStock.com, pp. 10, 23 (top left); © mediaphotos/iStock.com, p. 13; © stellalevi/iStock.com, pp. 14–15, 23 (top right); © Veronika Surovtseva/iStock.com, pp. 17, 23 (bottom left); © vitapix/iStock.com, p. 19; © Monkey Business Images/Shutterstock.com, pp. 20–21; © Donnay Style/Shutterstock.com, p. 22.

Front Cover: © Yellowj/Shutterstock.com.